T0197589

Three Bears, Two Moose, and a Rainbow

Ginny Grossman

WestBow Press books may be ordered through booksellers or by contacting:

WestBow Press
A Division of Thomas Nelson & Zondervan
1663 Liberty Drive
Bloomington, IN 47403
www.westbowpress.com
844-714-3454

ISBN: 978-1-4908-7648-1 (sc)
ISBN: 978-1-4908-7649-8 (e)

Library of Congress Control Number: 2015905917

Print information available on the last page.

WestBow Press rev. date: 06/15/2022

WestBow
PRESS®
A DIVISION OF THOMAS NELSON
& ZONDERVAN

Dedicated
To

My Heavenly Father, and to introducing His Word to as many young children as possible.

There was a Mama bear and her twin cubs that lived in the mountains of Montana. They were on their way to meet their best friends Mrs. Moose and her calf Calvin.

Love one another deeply from the heart.
1 Peter 1:22 NIV

It was a beautiful day and they were going to meet them at Rainbow Cove for a picnic, their favorite place for picnics.

Make the most of every opportunity.
Colossians 4:5 NIV

On their journey the cubs rolled down steep hills doing somersaults, laughing until their tummies hurt.

Be joyful always.
1 Thessalonians 5:16 NIV

Picking wild blueberries and huckleberries as they went and, of course, tasting them to make sure the berries were good enough for their friends.

And do not forget to do good and share with others, for with such sacrifices God is pleased. Hebrews 13:16 NIV

They caught fresh fish while crossing chilly streams, splashing, giggling, and playing hide and seek behind bushes.

Always give thanks to God the
Father for everything.
Ephesians 5:20 NIV

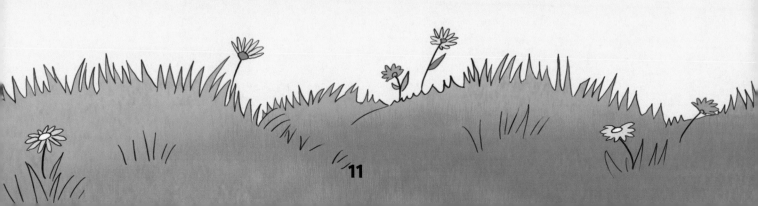

The cubs were so excited and couldn't wait to see Calvin and his mom. Suddenly, there were big dark clouds and it started to rain. The cubs started crying because they were sure the picnic would be canceled.

You too, be patient and stand firm.
James 5:8 NIV

Mama bear being very wise dried their eyes and gave them a big bear hug. She told them they would go to the picnic as planned because by the time they reached the cove the rain will probably be gone.

Love each other as I have loved you.
John 15:12 NIV

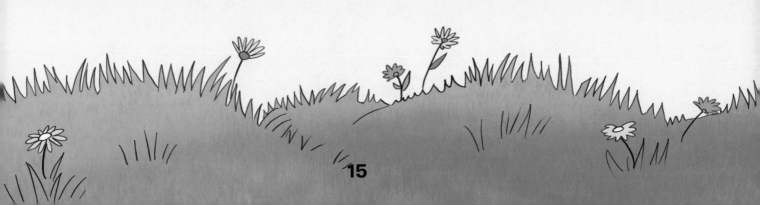

That's just what they did and Mama bear was right. As soon as they reached Rainbow Cove the rain stopped. The bears were sure the rain stopped just for them.

Show the wonder of Your great love.
Psalm 17:7 NIV

The sun came out and there was a beautiful rainbow right above their heads. The cubs and Calvin danced and played, and had a wonderful picnic. They all gave thanks to God for the beautiful day and their blessings.

Let the beauty of the Lord our God be upon us.
Psalm 90:17 NIV

Printed in the United States
by Baker & Taylor Publisher Services